LifeCaps

Vuitton

A Biography of Louis Vuitton

By Fergus Mason

■BOOKCAPS

BookCaps™ Study Guides

www.bookcaps.com

© 2015. All Rights Reserved.

Table of Contents

ABOUT LIFECAPS 3

INTRODUCTION 4

CHAPTER 1 9

CHAPTER 2 24

CHAPTER 3 33

CHAPTER 4 40

CHAPTER 5 55

CHAPTER 6 76

CHAPTER 7 87

CHAPTER 8 97

CONCLUSION 103

About LifeCaps

LifeCaps is an imprint of BookCaps™ Study Guides. With each book, a lesser known or sometimes forgotten life is recapped. We publish a wide array of topics (from baseball and music to literature and philosophy), so check our growing catalogue regularly (www.bookcaps.com) to see our newest books.

Introduction

We're all familiar with the top designer brands; their clothes, handbags, sunglasses and accessories regularly drape the forms of celebrities, their slick marketing fills the pages of glossy magazines and Hollywood studios compete fiercely for product placement deals. For many the luxury goods they sell are an aspiration, something they want to own as a tangible measure of success. For others they seem unattainable, something from another world that can only be looked at from afar. To almost everyone except some dedicated anti-capitalists they carry an air of glamor, and their appeal is so great that a whole huge industry exists to make unlicensed fakes; spend a day wandering through Istanbul's Grand Bazaar, or any market in the Far East, and you'll see tables piled high with Dolce & Gabbana bags, Jimmy Choo shoes and Versace sunglasses – all counterfeit, but ranging from obvious fakes that sell at knockdown prices and wouldn't fool anyone except in very dim light, to high quality ones that are almost works of art in their own right and can cost more than half what the originals do. Designer label goods don't usually do the job much better than more mainstream equivalents of course, and if you just want a handbag that will look smart and carry all your stuff a relatively cheap one is all you need. Even so demand for the big names remains high, and they show no sign of losing their attractiveness. Even economic downturns don't harm their sales much; the people who can afford to buy them don't usually have to count their pennies just because the global economy has tanked.

So much attention gets focused on designer goods and the powerful companies who make them that it's easy to forget these brands mostly once were the product of a single man or woman with a vision. There's a reason they're mostly named after one or two people; that's because, in the beginning, one creative genius came up with a product that changed the way things were done. Some of these founders came from privileged backgrounds; Christian Dior was the son of a wealthy industrialist whose first job was running a Bohemian art gallery. Domenico Dolce was a fashion college dropout and Stefano Gabbana was an aspiring sportswear designer. Dolce had originally tried to get a job working for Giorgio Armani, who also came from a wealthy family. Armani planned to become a doctor but after three years of medical school he got bored and, after a few years in the army, drifted into the fashion industry. Other companies have more sinister origins. Hugo Boss is one of the largest fashion houses today but its founder, Hugo Boss himself, was an enthusiastic member of the Nazi Party and the SS. His company manufactured uniforms for the SS and *Wehrmacht*, and from 1939 to 1945 used slave labor in its factories. After the war Boss was heavily fined and stripped of the right to vote.

And then there are some companies that were created from nothing by one man with no wealth but a ton of vision. The most remarkable of these has to be Louis Vuitton. Born into grinding poverty in rural France, he worked his way to the top of the luggage industry through sheer hard work and raw talent. In the early years of his life he seemed destined to become an agricultural laborer or manual tradesman, but his ambitions were a lot bigger than that. As a teenager he set out to develop the skills he needed to take on a competitive trade and emerge as the winner. In the process he built a reputation for workmanship that let him strike out on his own and build his workshop into an international brand that's still a world leader today, more than a century and a half after he founded it. Most remarkable of all, some of its products are almost unchanged from that time – but, thanks to their timeless design and unbeatable quality, they still sell in the very different world of the 21st century. Here is Louis Vuitton's incredible story.

Chapter 1

Anchay, in the Jura region of southeastern France, hardly even qualifies as a village. It's nothing more than a loose collection of farms and cottages, strung out for less than a quarter of a mile along the road between Bourg-en-Bresse and Lons-le-Saunier. There isn't even an inn or a village store, just a couple of dozen scattered buildings. Some of them are modern; most are old, built from irregular blocks of local stone covered in a layer of rough plaster. White-painted wooden shutters hang in front of many windows, protection against the winter cold. Anchay is surrounded on three sides by wooded hills and it's a long way from the coast, so winters there are harsh and snow often blocks the roads. It isn't much like Paris or the resorts along the Mediterranean coast. This is an agricultural area and the people are stereotypical French farmers – conservative, insular and suspicious of outsiders. The French language didn't fully replace the ancient Arpitan tongue until well into the 20th century and in remote villages the old speech can still sometimes be heard even today.

Time hasn't completely passed Anchay by. The road is paved and cars sit outside every home; the first house you pass as you enter the village from the south has a satellite dish bolted to the chimney and a twelve-foot pool set up in the yard. Look around as the light fades, though, and you can easily picture it as it was nearly two centuries ago. Of course back then life was even harder, with no electricity or running water. Light came from candles or oil lamps, and heat from wood stoves. Spring was the planting season; in summer and fall the people labored to get in enough food and fuel to last them through the winter. It was a hard, grinding existence and the horizons were very close; for many people a visit to the market in Thoirette, six miles down the road, was as far as they ever traveled. It was no place to live if your ambitions stretched further than scraping a living from the land.

Louis Vuitton was born in a local midwife's house in Lavans-sur-Valouse, three quarters of a mile west of Anchay, on August 4, 1821. The Vuitton family had lived in and around the village for generations and was solidly part of the area's working class; their ancestors had worked as builders and carpenters as well as on the land. His father Xavier was a miller[i] who also owned a small farm and his mother, Corinne, was a milliner. There was no real industry in the village – there still isn't – but Corinne sewed and shaped hats at home. Once every week or so the local hat merchant would come by in his cart, collect what she'd made and pay her. Many women in rural areas supplemented the farm income by making hats, clothing or similar items; a few large clothing factories did exist, mostly making uniforms for the military, but small-scale manufacture ruled everywhere outside the major cities. That was a blessing for the farmers, who struggled to earn a living from the rough land. The region's economy was based on wine just as it is today, with vineyards covering the lower part of any south-facing slope, but small general farmers were also required to supply the local markets with vegetables, dairy products and meat. After they'd produced enough for their own needs there was often little left to sell and having another income often made the difference between survival and bankruptcy.

For a young boy it could be a hard life. At a young age Louis Vuitton would have been given his share of chores around the farm. As soon as he could walk he would have toddled around after Corinne as she fed the chickens and milked the family cows; later his father would take him to work in the fields. Work on the farm would have begun just after dawn and lasted until dusk, while Corinne used the precious daylight to make hats – sewing by candlelight was difficult. In fact, until gas lighting became common there were serious restrictions on what people could do after dark – even reading by lamp or candle light isn't easy.

There are no records left that say whether or not Louis went to school. It's unlikely. Even today Anchay is far too small to have a school, and in fact the nearest one is five miles away in Arinthod. In theory, France has had compulsory education up to age 14 since 1698 – at least for boys – but in practice it was widely ignored in rural areas. Village schools were mandated by law but many children simply didn't attend. When Louis was born France was still recovering from the long ordeal of the Napoleonic Wars, which had devastated the economy through excessive military spending and the loss of hundreds of thousands of workers to war, famine and disease. Many farming families simply couldn't spare their children from work.

As Louis grew people began to notice that he had a strong personality and a streak of stubbornness. He seemed to find life on the farm boring. He had a point, as the days passed in a monotonous routine of hard work in the fields and outbuildings. Every year ran to a fixed calendar of planting, tending and harvesting crops; animals were raised, from calving and lambing in spring to the October sale or slaughter of the ones who wouldn't be kept through the winter. Firewood was stockpiled, and then burned, in a never-ending cycle. For a boy with ambitions Anchay had little to offer.

When Louis was ten, his mother died. That was far from rare. Today France has a higher life expectancy than the USA (81.6 years, against 79.5) but in 1831 it was much lower. On average a Frenchwoman born at the turn of the 19th century could expect to live for just 30 years.[ii] Of course that figure was distorted by the high rate of infant mortality – nearly half of children died before the age of ten – but there were plenty hazards for adults as well. Farmyards are dirty places and infections were common; without antibiotics those, and many diseases that today are easily treated, were almost universally lethal. Even in a tiny settlement like Anchay deaths would have been a depressingly regular event. It isn't known exactly how Corinne Vuitton died, but it's possible to take an educated guess.

Cholera is a bacterial disease – treatable with antibiotics – that spreads through contaminated water. Today it's associated with the developing world but in the 19th century it was a global problem. The development of proper sewer systems and treated drinking water has almost eliminated it in the west but those are modern developments, and before they became commonplace cholera epidemics regularly flared up throughout Europe and North America. A series of six huge pandemics caused millions of deaths in 19th century Europe – the mass graves dug for victims can still often be seen in many towns – and the second of these swept through France and Western Europe in 1831. More than a hundred thousand people died in France alone. The big cities with their crude sewers and public water pumps were worst affected but the disease soon spread out into the countryside too.

There was no running water supply in Anchay and the people took their water either from wells or from the tiny stream, barely more than a drainage ditch today, that runs down into the village. Untreated cholera victims usually die of dehydration caused by massive diarrhea and vomiting; up to five gallons of diarrhea can be produced every day, and it's loaded with the bacteria. All it would take was a carelessly discarded chamber pot splashing into the stream, or a victim's soiled clothing being rinsed out, to pass the plague on. Did Corinne die after drinking contaminated water? No records survive to give us a hint, but it's very possible. Cholera was certainly the leading cause of death in France that year.

Whatever his wife had died of, Xavier Vuitton didn't stay a widower for long. It was common at the time for people to quickly remarry after the death of a spouse. Often it was a pragmatic decision; widows gained some financial security by marrying again, while men would have someone to take care of their home and children while they worked. Many of these second marriages worked out very well. Because so many mothers died in childbirth these unions often lasted far longer than either spouse's first marriage. Xavier's seems to have been less successful, though. Louis formed an immediate dislike for his new stepmother and in turn her attempts to control him made the situation worse. The boy became increasingly frustrated and unhappy, and added to his existing frustration with village life this made him start to think about heading out into the wider world. But he was still too young, and for the next three years he endured a miserable existence on the farm. He didn't always suffer in silence; his stubbornness led to frequent clashes with his stepmother.

When he was thirteen Louis had had enough. For months the family had been penned up in the house by the winter, and that had just made the conflicts worse. Xavier Vuitton showed no signs of divorcing his new wife – local legend tends to back up Louis's dislike of her, portraying her as a strict and domineering woman, but Xavier seemed content enough – and finally the boy decided his only option was to get away and seek his fortune somewhere else. As the winter slowly eased he waited impatiently. The snow melted from the valleys, then the hills, to be followed by the spring rain. The dirt roads of the region turned to mud and the fields and forests were soaked for a few weeks. Then finally the sun reappeared and the land began to dry out. On the first good day of spring in 1835 Louis, still only thirteen, quietly slipped away from the farmhouse without a word of farewell and set out for Paris.

From Anchay to Paris is about 225 miles as the crow flies; by road it's closer to 295. Walking steadily that would take about three weeks. It took Louis much longer. He had no food or money, so his progress was slow and haphazard. At each farm or village along the way he would offer to do odd jobs, in exchange for a meal or cash. Such wandering vagrants were common in France at the time. Thousands of demobilized veterans of Napoleon's wars were still roaming the country two decades later, surviving by doing casual labor for farmers or artisans. Now Louis joined them. It wasn't an easy life but it was certainly possible to survive that way. Even today many farms hire in casual workers for the harvest season, and before agriculture became mechanized there was a huge demand for seasonal workers. The rest of the year a wanderer could still find work clearing drainage ditches, herding livestock or hoeing vegetable plots. Raised on a farm himself, Louis knew how to do all these jobs. As he traveled he would have learned the skills of a handyman, too. The more things he could turn his hand to the better his chances of finding work, so he had a real incentive to pick up all the practical knowledge he could.

Sometimes he worked a few hours in exchange for a meal or a few coins. At harvest he might stay on a farm for days or even weeks, lodging in the barn with the other hired men and earning a small wage. Other times he found himself sleeping in the woods, wrapped in his cloak. When he couldn't find work he lived on whatever cash he'd managed to save. Month after month he meandered across southeastern France, always drifting in the direction of the capital. As he went he found odd jobs with artisans and craftsmen of every type, learning to do basic work with metal, stone, fabrics and wood. Some of this experience would be very useful to him later.

As he moved north Louis started to come across larger towns. He had grown up in a tiny village of a few dozen people; the largest place he'd ever seen was probably Arinthod, with a population of less than 200 at the time. Now he came to Dijon, capital of the Côte D'Or region and home to almost 25,000 people. Dijon was still in a wine-making region like Anchay but it was also a center of science and education, with a university founded in 1722, and all the industries needed to support a large town. The city attracted artists and scholars as well as poor farmers, and as Louis wandered the streets with his few belongings in an old sack he saw porters unloading the heavy leather trunks of the wealthy outside homes and hotels.

After Dijon came Troyes, a smaller city with a thriving textile industry; again he worked at odd jobs, picking up new skills. Perhaps he spent the winter there before setting out on the final leg of the journey. In any case, in 1837 he finally reached his destination – Paris.

Chapter 2

If the towns he'd visited along the way had impressed Louis, Paris must have been a shock. The capital of France already had a population of close to a million, and it was one of the most visited cities in Europe. It was about to get a lot bigger – that year the first railway line to the city was opened, bringing an influx of immigrants from rural France. Some, like Louis, came because they were bored; others were looking for a job.

Paris was founded in the 3rd century BC, and for most of its existence its markets had been supplied by local tradesmen. By the 1830s that was beginning to change. The Industrial Revolution had begun in England in the early 1760s, and spread to France around half a century later. By the time Louis reached Paris the city's traditional workshops were being joined, and later replaced, by bigger and more modern factories. These produced goods on a much larger scale and exported them around the French empire and the rest of the world, so they also needed a larger workforce. These new workers came from the rural areas, in turn motivating farmers to adopt more machinery as their labor pool shrank. Louis wasn't the only farm boy looking for a job in Paris, but luckily there were plenty of vacancies.

Even in pre-industrial times Paris had been famous for its fashions; by the 1830s the French aristocracy was returning to prominence now that the Revolution had faded away and Napoleon was gone, and French styles were as popular as ever. Paris was part of the Grand Tour that young rich people made. It was a cultural as well as industrial capital and there was a lot of wealth floating around. That attracted even more businesses, providing high quality goods, and positions in those companies were very desirable. Louis got lucky though; not long after arriving in Paris he was taken on as an apprentice box maker and packer.

We make jokes about how much people pack for a vacation, but the reality is that modern travel is stripped down and minimalist compared to 180 years ago. Luggage is compact and mass produced, and often what we can take with us is restricted by airline weight limits. It was very different for the 19th century rich. They traveled by carriage or ship; often they stayed with friends or in large hotels with much more spacious rooms, and they could – and did – take a lot of luggage with them. As well as clothes there would be an assortment of bulky hats, shoes and grooming items. If they were making an extended trip people would often take ornaments, paintings, musical instruments and even small pieces of furniture with them. All of this had to be packed to stand long journeys over bumpy roads or in the hold of a ship, and the aristocracy weren't going to cram it into mass-produced suitcases. Instead, they used trunks for their clothes and boxes for everything else. The highest quality boxes were custom made to fit the objects they would contain, and often finished to a very high quality. The box maker's company would then personally pack the items when their client traveled, and unpack them again on their return. It was a respected trade, and craftsmen like Monsieur Marechal were valued members of the growing middle class.

Marechal took Louis Vuitton on as an apprentice in 1837, and began teaching him the tricks of the trade. The main material for boxes was leather, because it was fairly water resistant and gave good protection to its contents. To maintain shape it was attached to a wooden frame. Farming involves a lot of basic carpentry – gates need to be repaired, and stalls built for animals – but now Louis had to learn a completely new set of skills. The box frames were much finer and more complicated than anything he'd ever made before, and the standard of finish had to be far higher. Then there was the art of cutting and fitting the leather covers, followed by the shaped interior lining that would hold the contents securely.

At first, like most apprentices, Louis watched the craftsmen work between doing odd jobs in Marechal's workshop. Like most apprentices he learned where everything was by sweeping around it, and got to know the staff by running errands for them. Then Marechal and his senior workers started introducing the teenager to the skills he would need. He watched them as they worked, then was given scraps of material to practice the techniques on. Once they were happy that he knew what he was doing he started to work on actual boxes under close supervision. Marechal would cut the pieces of the frame then let Louis glue and nail them together; then he would help work out the measurements and teach Louis how to cut the wood himself. After a few dozen frames had worked out successfully the master craftsman stood back and watched as Louis did the next one himself, although for several months longer he or one of his deputies would carefully check the boy's work. Then it was on to making the leather covers, and the whole process would start again.

There was more to learn than just making boxes. Part of Marechal's service included packing the contents for transport and that was an art in itself. Louis was carefully taught how to fold clothes for packing, and how to handle delicate objects without breaking them or marking the finish. He wasn't quite ready to go out on packing jobs just yet though.

Box makers and packers were respected tradesmen and often came into contact with the upper classes. That meant they had to meet the expected social standards, and Louis was still an unsophisticated farm boy. In addition to the details of his actual job he also had to learn how to deal with customers, and Marechal taught him that too. His country accent faded, replaced by a more sophisticated Paris one. Around the workshop he wore a plain woolen smock and heavy leather work shoes, but he was also fitted for a smart uniform in the livery of Marechal's shop. When the owner thought he was ready he started to go out on jobs, helping to pack items away in their boxes and load them onto carriages.

Being an apprentice was ideal for Louis. He didn't get paid much but there were many other benefits. The apprentice system in Europe was regulated by the powerful trade guilds and it had strict rules. Customers, especially wealthy ones, preferred to buy goods made by a master craftsman, but there were never enough master craftsmen to meet the demand. The guilds allowed their members to take on extra labor, usually young men, on low wages. In return the apprentices were given food, lodgings and training. After their apprenticeship – which usually lasted seven years – they became journeymen. Sometimes this meant continuing to work in the shop of a master craftsman; others were sent out to travel for up to three years, surviving by hiring out the skills they'd learned. This tradition still survives in Germany, where journeyman carpenters are given a traditional costume and €5 (about $7) and spend three years and a day earning a living by doing whatever carpentry work they can find. It was dying away in France, though, so once his apprenticeship was over Louis remained in Marechal's workshop. He had one thing left to do before he was a master craftsman in his own right; he had to make a masterpiece – a demonstration that would be presented to the guild. If they approved it he would be qualified as a master. In the meantime he worked on, earning a proper wage making goods for Marechal to sell. Louis quickly became a favorite of Marechal's aristocratic clients, but his big break came when he was selected by the most important woman in France.

Chapter 3

For a while it seemed that the Anglo-Prussian defeat of Napoleon Bonaparte in 1815 had closed the book on the French Revolution, with the Bourbon monarchy restored to power and the surviving members of Napoleon's family in exile. The discontent that had led to the revolution still bubbled under the surface though, and the excesses of earlier kings hadn't been forgotten. When Louis XVIII died in 1824 he was succeeded by his brother Charles X, who immediately started passing a series of unpopular laws. Two of them stood out. The first, prompted by Charles's close links with the church, was the imposition of the death penalty for anyone who interfered with communion wafers. This violated the separation of church and state laid down in the French constitution. Secondly, he ordered compensation payments for anyone who had been declared an "enemy of the revolution" during the First Republic. Thousands of people had been persecuted by the revolutionaries but the new law would mainly have benefited Charles's aristocratic friends, at taxpayers' expense.

Both of these laws caused discontent, but instead of listening Charles responded by tightening censorship laws. Next, he dissolved the new French parliament and postponed elections. Finally, on July 25, 1830 he abolished the freedom of the press, dissolved parliament again and banned the middle class from voting in future elections (restricting voting to the aristocracy). That triggered a three-day revolution, with fighting in the streets of Paris; by July 29 Charles was fleeing to Britain and a provisional government was being formed.

After the July Revolution the French monarchy passed to the Orléans branch of the Bourbon family, traditionally seen as more liberal. The new king was Louis-Philippe I, and he was more popular than Charles X had been. He still favored the elite over the middle classes, though, and that was especially hard on small manufacturers like Marechal. Louis Vuitton, who had qualified as a master craftsman and was now a member of the middle class himself, was at a disadvantage; the voting laws left him disenfranchised and the power handed to bankers made it almost impossible for him to open his own business. Louis-Philippe was finally overthrown June 1848 and the long history of the French monarchy finally came to an end, replaced by the Second Republic. That didn't last long either, though. Presidential elections were set for October, and the winner would end the Republic within a few years.

Louis-Napoleon Bonaparte was the nephew of the famous Emperor Napoleon, and he'd spent most of his life in politically imposed exile in Switzerland or Britain. As ambitious as his uncle had been, he twice launched coups against the French monarchy; both were spectacular failures. When the Second Republic was declared, however, he decided his time had come. Returning to France he stood in the October elections and won overwhelmingly, partly thanks to his name, and became the first directly elected leader of France.

The constitution blocked Louis-Napoleon from standing for a second term, but rather than step down he launched a coup in 1851 then, next year, declared the second French Empire and appointed himself as Emperor Napoleon III (his father was counted as Napoleon II, even though he never used the title).

During his exile in London Louis-Napoleon had a series of widely publicized affairs; his lovers included the famous French actress Rachel and the English heiress Harriet Howard. However, after becoming emperor he started looking for a suitable wife, and in 1852 he met the 23-year-old Spanish noblewoman Eugénie de Montijo. They were married in January 1853 and Eugénie was installed as the Empress of France.

Napoleon III was a more popular ruler than the last two kings had been, but he still lived in a grand style. The Imperial family had several residences, including the Tuileries Palace in the city and the Château de Saint-Cloud three miles away; like many wealthy Parisians still do they usually abandoned the city in July and August, when it's often unpleasantly hot, and stayed at the Château. In between times they traveled around the country or throughout Europe. That meant they needed a lot of boxes and packing services, and Marechal's shop was one of the ones they used.

By now Louis was one of Marechal's leading employees, and his skill had become widely recognized. He was soon assigned to help with packing Eugénie's possessions when she was preparing to travel and quickly became her favorite. In 1853 she took the step of appointing him as her personal box maker and packer, with special responsibility for handling her extensive collection of clothes.[iii] That was a huge honor in itself, but more importantly it also opened all the doors he could have imagined. He had been personally hired by the Empress of France herself; that made his skills even more desirable, and fashionable women rushed to hire him.

His increased popularity was a huge boost for Marechal's shop, but Louis knew that he could now safely go into business for himself. With his services in so much demand he wouldn't lack clients, and he also had some ideas about how he could offer an even better service. His personal situation was about to change, too, giving him even more of an incentive to move on.

Chapter 4

Not long after being appointed as Empress Eugénie's personal packer, Louis met Clemence-Emilie Parriaux. By this time Louis was 32 years old and Emilie was only seventeen, but nevertheless the two soon fell in love. They married in 1854. A few months later Louis resigned from Marechal's shop to open his own.

The Place Vendôme is one of the most exclusive places in Paris. Located centrally, in the 1st Arrondissement, it's surrounded by high-class hotels and expensive apartments. The Place itself is an open paved area with an impressive, weathered copper column in the center, and the streets around it contained a variety of luxury stores. Louis managed to rent a vacant unit at 4 rue Neuve des Capucines and that's where he set up his first workshop. By now he was a skilled carpenter and with what he'd learned from working with Marechal he was also experienced at working with satin, silk and leather. That gave him the ability to produce any type of box or luggage in common use at the time, and all his products were beautifully made. Louis himself was already well known among the aristocracy and now, with his appointment to the empress, he was highly in demand. His new shop quickly became one of the most popular box makers in Paris. He capitalized on his association with the empress and hung a sign outside the shop: "Securely packs the most fragile objects. Specializing in packing fashions."[iv]

There was a reason he gave a special mention to packing fashions. The streets around the Place Vendôme also held many of France's – and that meant the world's – top couturiers. The most fashionable women in Europe came there to order new dresses, all of them tailor-made, and once they were ready they needed to be shipped to their new owners. Style ruled here with an iron rod, and what could be more stylish than to deliver your dresses in a box made by the personal box-maker to the empress? Louis picked up a lot of work from the couturiers,[v] and he acknowledged that on his sign.

At first Louis followed the same styles as Marechal and the other leading box makers, but he had ideas of his own about how the job should be done and before long he started putting them into practice. Trunks and packing boxes hadn't changed much in over a century but that was simply because of tradition. Industrialization was making new materials available, and changing fashions meant they could perhaps be made acceptable to buyers. One thing that Louis was keen to do was replace leather as a covering material. It had advantages; it was tough, and could survive the ravages of being transported. There were also drawbacks, though. It scuffed easily, and quickly became shabby unless it was constantly maintained. Unless it was kept well waxed or oiled leather wasn't very waterproof. If water was left to stand on a trunk it would eventually soak through. The material also tended to absorb odors then pass them on to its contents, and before the development of modern sewage systems – which didn't exist in Paris until well into Napoleon III's reign – there were plenty of odors around. In addition to that problem leather has its own distinctive smell, especially when it's been damp, and that also tended to transfer itself to the contents of a leather-bound trunk.

For his first few years as an independent maker Louis continued to make leather boxes, but he also began experimenting with other materials. Finally he settled on canvas. Most modern canvas is made from cotton but in the 19th century it was usually hemp or linen. It's a strong, heavy, tightly woven fabric that's already quite water resistant, even when untreated. However new treatments were becoming available that made it completely waterproof – and, unlike leather, it didn't have to be regularly retreated. It also wouldn't lose its waterproof properties if it was slightly scuffed, which was almost inevitable during transport. Louis tried various kinds of canvas until he found one that looked like the perfect solution, and made some experimental boxes covered with it. He quickly found out that it also had other advantages over leather. It was much lighter, for a start. It was more resistant to scuffing. It also lasted longer; unless well cared for leather dries out and becomes brittle, before finally crumbling. During a long voyage in the hold of a ship a leather trunk could deteriorate badly, and passengers often found their possessions damaged by seawater or tainted by the stench of the bilges. Canvas, however, didn't need any care beyond simple cleaning with a brush or damp cloth. It seemed to be the ideal material.

Louis's original plan was to simply substitute canvas for leather in his existing designs, and that worked fine for the smaller boxes. Then, as he began thinking about new trunks, an idea occurred to him. Traditional trunks were rectangular boxes with a rounded lid; the shape of the lid was chosen so that any water that landed on the trunk would run off, instead of lying there to soak through the leather. Unfortunately it also meant that trunks couldn't be stacked in a railway carriage or ship's hold; they could only be packed in one layer deep, then if necessary a platform of planks would be built to hold the next layer. That meant loading a ship was very time-consuming, but there was no alternative. Now perhaps there was. Lids were domed because of the properties of leather, but if the new trunks were to be canvas-covered that constraint didn't matter anymore.

Now he went to work making a new trunk with a simple, flat lid. This had several advantages. It was easier to make, for a start. The old shape needed semicircular wooden supports and these had to be laboriously bent in a steam box, a slow operation that needed a lot of skill. The new lid was a simple frame made from straight timber. Flat-topped trunks could be easily stacked on top of each other, meaning that more baggage could be fitted in a ship or railway wagon. A trunk with the new shape could hold as much as an old-style one while not being as high, because there was no wasted volume. The new design seemed to be better in every way, but would people buy it? It was radically different from what they were used to. Still, Louis was convinced that he had a better product. He set his staff to work making a selection of trunks and boxes to the new design, and in 1858 they went on sale.

Previous Louis Vuitton products had been well made and stylish, but conventional. Now Parisians who visited his shop saw something completely different. Old-fashioned brown leather was replaced with canvas in a smart color he called Trianon gray,[vi] giving the new luggage a clean, modern appearance. The corners and edges were trimmed with brass reinforcement, and wooden rubbing strips along the top, bottom and sides protected the canvas from scuffs or tears; that gave it its name, the slat trunk.[vii] Members of staff were on hand to demonstrate how the trunks could be stacked neatly on top of each other for easy loading, and they assured the customers that these new models were more robust than the old ones and would last longer with less maintenance. Some people were dubious but many others took the plunge, and by the end of 1858 the new Vuitton baggage was becoming a common sight in French society.

Within a year or two people were noticing the advantages of the canvas trunks, and demand began to increase rapidly. Before long Louis found that he was struggling to keep up. He was also busy at home; his son Georges had been born in 1857[viii]. Still, success was welcome and he started looking for a solution. It soon became obvious that his Paris shop was too small to cope with the volume of orders he was getting, and there was no easy way to expand. The solution was to move the manufacturing side of the business to a less central location. Since 1815 the population of Paris had doubled but the city's area had stayed the same; it was becoming extremely overcrowded. In an attempt to ease the problem Napoleon III annexed eleven surrounding towns to the city, creating a ring of suburbs. These quickly became the favored location for light industry and Louis was attracted to the possibilities they offered. He needed a presence in the city center, but property there was so expensive that he couldn't afford to run a large factory there. But if he split the factory from the shop he could have the best of both worlds.

He soon started to focus his search on Asnières-sur-Seine, about five miles northwest of the city center. This was the ideal location for him. It was easily accessible from the city, meaning his clients could still visit to order custom goods. Land was much cheaper so he could afford to build a larger workshop. It was also close to the river; as his popularity grew he was getting many export orders, and good access to the river made shipping easy. Bringing in materials was more convenient too – most of the wood he used came from the south of France, for example, and it could be brought down the Seine on barges. In 1859 he bought a large plot in Asnières and began building his new factory there. It gave him much more space to expand. The shop stayed in central Paris but his trunks were no longer made in the small workshop in the back; that was converted to a stock room and the premises became completely dedicated to the retail end of the business.

The plot in Asnières was also large enough to hold several houses, in addition to the factory, Louis built a home for himself and his family. It was a long way from the rough farmhouse in Anchay where he'd grown up; the success of his business had rapidly made him a wealthy man and he was able to afford a large, elegant house. Built in Art Nouveau style, with stained glass windows and colored accents in its brick walls, it boasted a library, billiard room and artistic garden.[ix] Louis filled it with classic furniture and antiques, but he probably didn't have as much time to enjoy it as he might have liked. Word of his new designs continued to spread through the upper reaches of French society, and his orders book was filling up faster than ever. The patronage of the empress made his products acceptable to anyone, even royalty, and his high-profile clients included the Khedive of Egypt.[x]

In fact, the Khedive was his first royal client outside the imperial family. He approached Louis because one of the greatest engineering achievements of the time – the Suez Canal – was about to be opened and as the semi-independent ruler of British-aligned Egypt he would be playing a part in the opening ceremony. The plan was for Empress Eugénie and the Khedive to make the first passage through the canal on the French imperial yacht *L'Aigle*. Pasha wanted to build closer relations between Egypt and France, so it was important for him to make a good impression on the stylish Spaniard. Wanting to cover every detail, he ordered a complete new set of travel accessories for the occasion. It was already well known that Eugénie had been buying her luggage from Vuitton for years, so Pasha could be sure that she would approve of his good taste.

In the end his efforts were upstaged. The Canal was a mostly French project, but Egypt was loosely aligned with the British Empire and many in Britain were annoyed that the French were hogging the attention the world's press had focused on the project. The opening ceremony was to take place on November 17, 1869 and on the night of the 16th a mass of ships assembled in the Mediterranean, ready to make history by sailing through the canal on its first day of operation. *L'Aigle* was in pride of place at the head of the line with Eugénie and Pasha on board, each comfortably maintained by their Vuitton luggage. During the night, however, another ship came gliding unnoticed through the anchored fleet under silent sails, with its engines shut down and its navigation lights doused. When dawn broke the various dignitaries were horrified to see the 570-ton gunboat HMS *Newport* neatly moored in front of *L'Aigle*, right at the mouth of the Canal. There was no room to pass her so the first vessel through the Canal, sending a powerful message about who really controlled things in the Middle East, was a British warship. Commander George Nares was publicly reprimanded for the stunt by the Royal Navy, but privately congratulated for his very visible flag-waving and outstanding seamanship in weaving through the packed shipping in the dark.[xi] Thanks to all the diplomatic fuss nobody was very interested in who had made the Khedive's luggage.

Chapter 5

The late 19th century was a period of innovation, and countries started to organize huge fairs to showcase their products. The first was the Great Exhibition, held in London in 1851. The aim was to display industrial products from around the world, and many Europeans were impressed at the range and quality of US-made goods on display, but the highlight was the exhibition building itself. The Crystal Palace was purpose-built for the event and nothing like it had ever been seen before; it was a huge prefabricated structure of glass and cast iron frames, more than 1,800 feet long and 128 feet high. The world was stunned by this display of British industrial power but France, never a country to happily accept second place, was determined to outdo their old rival. Paris hosted the next world's fair, in 1855, and turned it into a celebration of French luxury goods. The third fair was in 1862, in London, then in 1867 it was Paris's turn again.

The International Exhibition of 1867 was the largest world's fair yet. It was built on the Champ du Mars, the great military parade ground – now a public park – that stretches from the military academy to the banks of the River Seine. Through the summer of 1867 and into late fall it was dominated by the enormous exhibition center. A giant oval, built in the shape of a Roman circus, it was 1,608 feet long and 1,247 feet wide. Most of the interior was filled with galleries of small stands, surrounding a central pavilion and garden. The stands were filled with exhibitors from 42 countries, 52,000 of them in all, and many of them were dedicated to high-quality French products. One of the stallholders was Louis Vuitton.

Up to now Louis had been attracting new business mostly through word of mouth, and it had been incredibly successful; he was now generally accepted as the leading luggage maker in Paris. Now, suddenly, his work found an international audience. Over the seven months of the expedition it attracted more than six million visitors from around the world. The exhibits they saw included elaborate clocks, displays of recently discovered prehistoric tools and demonstrations of early electric devices, but one of the most talked about stands was Louis and his collection of revolutionary luggage. Many of the visitors were regular travelers; a very high percentage of those who'd come from abroad were wealthy or at least part of the affluent middle class, and the stylish trunks attracted a huge amount of interest.

Louis's skill, and the popularity of his designs, didn't go unrecognized. The exhibition committee awarded medals to the most innovative and successful exhibits. Of course the competition was stiff, with major scientific breakthroughs on display as well as new industrial processes and medical innovations. Still, Louis managed to win the bronze medal.[xii] It was an incredible endorsement and removed any doubt; he was now the leading baggage maker in France, and probably the world.

Following the exhibition demand for Vuitton trunks grew even more, and the business went from strength to strength. Unknown to Louis, however, there was trouble on the horizon. Within a few short years his business would be destroyed, not by an upstart rival but by war.

Otto von Bismarck, Chancellor of Prussia, had a mission. For centuries France, with its powerful army, had dominated - and often terrorized – mainland Europe. Meanwhile, the German-speaking people to the east were split into a loose collection of small, poor and often chaotic states. Bismarck believed that a properly organized German nation could act as a counterbalance to French influence, but the problem was persuading the princes, dukes and other leaders to give up their own small authority in exchange for being part of a great power. Like many leaders before him he decided the best way to get their attention was by creating an external threat, and what better enemy than France?

In 1870 Bismarck carefully manipulated a diplomatic crisis around the succession to the Spanish throne to make it appear that Prussia had insulted France. Driven by media pressure the French parliament began demanding war with Prussia and Napoleon III, confident that the French Empire could defeat Prussia and its allies in the North German Confederation, couldn't resist the temptation. On July 16, 1870 the government of France voted to declare war on the Germans and began to mobilize their army. But Napoleon had walked right into a trap; the Prussians were eager for war and their own army, superbly trained and famously disciplined, was already fully mobilized.

France had a larger regular army than the North Germans – 492,000 men against only 300,000 – but the Prussians also had an enormous reserve of close to a million trained men, which far outnumbered the French *Garde Mobile*. The southern German states, alarmed by French moves near their borders just as Bismarck had planned, also began mobilizing. Then, on July 31, the French army crossed the border and advanced on Saarbrücken under Napoleon III's personal command. The war seemed to be going well for France, but then they heard reports of three separate Prussian armies closing in on them. Alarmed, Napoleon retreated back into France. On August 4 the Prussian onslaught rolled across the border.

The French were generally better equipped than their enemies, with their more modern rifles giving them a real advantage, but Prussian leadership and discipline was far superior and the French armies were quickly driven back in a series of stunning defeats. Napoleon III was captured at the Battle of Sedan on September 2, and by the middle of the month Prussian forces were closing in on Paris. The city's defense relied on a ring of outlying forts – which the Prussians quickly captured – and the 21-mile-long Thiers Wall. The center of Paris was inside the Wall. Louis's workshop in Asnières wasn't. On September 19 the Prussian ring closed around Paris and Louis, with his family, fled into the city.

Bismarck wanted his artillery to shell the city to speed up its surrender, but the Prussian generals refused. That would be a violation of the rules of war, they told him, and anyway it would actually make it harder to destroy the remaining French armies. They were right; thousands of French troops were thrown away in attempts to break the siege, while roving Prussian columns defeated most of the surviving French generals. Despite breakout attempts by its defenders Paris was cut off, with hot air balloons the only way its inhabitants could communicate with the unoccupied regions of France.

Paris had several major markets supplied by the surrounding countryside, so at first there was plenty of food. As the siege dragged on through October and into winter, however, stockpiles began to run low. Horses were slaughtered for food, then pets, rats and all the animals from the Paris Zoo (including two elephants). A rather alarming restaurant menu from December 1870 offers cat with rats, kangaroo, elephant soup and stuffed donkey's head.[xiii] By the end of the year almost everything in Paris that could be eaten had been. For Louis and his family, crammed into temporary accommodation with thousands of other refugees, it was a rude awakening. He'd escaped the grind of rural life and achieved wealth, fame and success, but now he was starving just like everyone else in the city.

Things were bad for the residents of Paris, but they weren't a lot better for the besieging troops. Because everything they needed had to be brought from Germany the Prussian army was often short of supplies, especially food, and after months of cold weather the army that ringed Paris was starting to suffer. Many of the men were becoming ill with tuberculosis and food was strictly rationed. Finally, in January, Bismarck managed to override the objections of his generals and got his way; to bring the siege to an end before the army weakened any more Paris would be shelled. The army had heavy Krupp siege guns, built for blasting a path through city defenses, and on January 25 they opened fire. Terror quickly spread through Paris as the huge shells blasted whole streets into rubble. The defenders were too weak and exhausted to attempt another breakout, and the city's commander was soon forced to admit defeat. On January 28, after three days of shelling, Paris surrendered and the Prussians moved in. On February 6 the remains of the

French army agreed a ceasefire and the war was over.

The rapid Prussian victory persuaded the other German states that they were better off as part of a larger nation, and the official unification of Germany took place even before shells started falling on Paris. With that, and the extraction of 5.5 billion gold francs ($19.2 billion in 2014 dollars) in war reparations from France, the Prussians were satisfied; they weren't interested in annexing France and when the last reparation payment was handed over in September 1873 they withdrew their troops. In fact, they had abandoned Paris as early as mid-February 1871, after holding a victory parade. Unfortunately, the power vacuum soon led to chaos.

Leftists in Paris had become increasingly restless during the siege and had already tried to seize power twice. In March 1871, after the Prussian armies pulled out of the city, they tried again. This time, two army generals were killed by national guardsmen loyal to the socialist Paris Commune, and fighting broke out between government troops and armed socialist militias. By late March, the city was under the control of the Commune, and a new socialist regime was developing. The French government wasn't going to accept the loss of its capital, though, and after a delay of a few weeks to rebuild its shattered forces the army fought its way back into the city. The Commune was defeated on May 28 and Paris came back under government control. The bitter street fighting in late May had done almost as much damage as the Prussian guns, and large areas of Paris were scarred by burned or demolished buildings.

When Louis made his way back to the factory at Asnières he found a scene of devastation. The district had been occupied by the Prussians during the siege, and their troops had stripped it of everything useful. Wood and furniture had been used for firewood, while his stockpile of waterproof, high quality canvas had been stolen by enterprising soldiers and used to make shelters. The factory, which had been working at full capacity less than a year before, was now just a shell.

Luckily for Louis he had saved enough money to start again, and he didn't waste any time. Workmen were hired and soon the factory was being rebuilt, with enlarged and modernized workshops that could handle the increased demand he anticipated. At the same time he decided to take the chance to find a new city center shop. The existing one was convenient for the dressmakers in the area, but it was small and there wasn't any room to expand. Until the war had interrupted him business had been growing at an impressive rate, and now that peace had returned he expected that to continue. Now, while the country got its breath back and came to terms with the defeat, he had a brief window of opportunity. The shop had been closed since the siege began; it would stay closed until the factory was ready to restart production. Now he had a chance to find a bigger shop while property prices were still depressed by the war, and he took it. He soon found vacant premises in an upscale district that were large enough to display his expanding product range, and immediately set about getting his business up and running again.

The new Louis Vuitton shop at 1 Rue Scribe was much more visible than the old one had been.[xiv] Located on a busy street filled with high-class hotels, boutiques and the famous Jockey Club, it was perfectly placed to attract the sort of customers Louis was looking for – and it did. Within months of reopening business was thriving again, and once more orders were coming in from all over the world.

Now Louis had more new ideas he wanted to try out. Up to now luggage had been very utilitarian; materials had been chosen for practicality rather than looks, and the traditional leather style had a dark, heavy look. Even Louis's canvas models were more practical than stylish; the gray color was at least partly a result of applying waterproofing compounds to white cloth. Canvas wasn't leather though. It was a fabric, and techniques for making patterned fabric had already been in use for centuries. Now the latest printing technology meant custom patterns could be produced on an industrial scale. It would be easy to cover a trunk with patterned canvas and give it a completely different appearance; fashionable travelers might like to own such distinctive baggage. Louis started trying out various patterns, aiming to produce a piece of luggage that was just as attractive as it was functional.

The new line was launched a year after the new workshop opened, in 1872. While the basic design was the same as his original slat trunk the canvas covering was now also available in a striped pattern. Two color schemes were available – red and beige, or brown and beige. They immediately generated a huge amount of interest; because they were so visibly different from older trunks they gave people a way to stand out and show how up to date they were. They also stood out as being original Vuitton products, because the original canvas models were already starting to suffer from a problem that still exists today – copying.

There were many luggage makers in Paris, and hundreds more throughout Europe and the USA. All of them were competing for a limited amount of business and a canvas-covered stackable trunk wasn't hard to make. Many competitors were skeptical of what Louis had done, but when they saw how popular his new designs were that changed rapidly and copies began to appear. After all, anybody who could make a domed leather trunk could make a flat-topped canvas one just as easily. By changing to the striped canvas Louis hoped he could set his own products apart from the competition for a while, but copying was a problem that would plague him for the rest of his life. His son eventually introduced the distinctive LV monogram in an attempt to end the problem, but that just shifted the focus from sincere imitations to outright fakes.

As the 19th century went on, changing tastes started to affect Louis's product range. The growing middle class wanted to travel, but they weren't looking for custom boxes as much as the aristocracy had been; instead they needed trunks and smaller, more easily handled luggage. Suitcases became increasingly popular and Louis soon started making them. It was an easy step, because they were made in the same way as a trunk – canvas over a wooden frame, usually reinforced with brass at the corners. They were also much more affordable than a trunk, which increased demand even more. Soft luggage was added to the Vuitton catalog – duffle bags and overnight bags were popular for rail journeys, which were rapidly replacing road travel for many people. Now it was possible to buy a matching set of Vuitton luggage, all made from the same striped canvas. Then Louis discovered another item that he thought might be popular.

Chapter 6

For all of recorded history men and women have needed some way to carry small possessions around with them. The Romans often concealed a small bag in the folds of a tunic or toga. In the Middle Ages everyone had one or more pouches fastened to their belt. Later men started carrying their belongings in their pockets, but that left women with a problem. In the late 18th century the reticule became popular in France, and later in Britain; this was a small pouch, usually made of silk, with a wrist strap. It was large enough to carry some coins but not much else.

Then, during the Industrial Revolution, railway lines started to spread – first across Britain, then throughout Europe. Before long railways were running in the USA, India, Egypt and southern Africa as well. With them came the concept of mass transit. Until then most people had spent their entire lives within twenty miles of their birthplace but suddenly it was easy to travel long distances quickly, without the enormous expense of hiring a coach and paying for frequent changes of horses.

There were disadvantages of course. A small group traveling in a coach had plenty of space for all the luggage they wanted – trunks and bags could be stacked on the roof. That wasn't going to work on a train, and while trains had baggage wagons the majority of the space was allocated to first class passengers. Quickly identifying the problem, Louis developed smaller and more affordable bags that were still large enough for the new middle and working class travelers. That fueled a general boom in luggage sales, but it also identified problems – especially for women. When English industrialist Samuel Parkinson ordered a set of matching traveling gear he decided that all the available purses and reticles for women were too small to carry his wife's everyday essentials, so he asked for a selection of larger bags as well. H.J. Cave, a London bag maker (who had won the gold medal at the 1867 Paris exhibition when Louis won the bronze) made some experimental designs then supplied Parkinson with several compact bags, each large enough to carry money, makeup and other small items. That marked the invention of what's now an essential fashion accessory – the handbag.

Surprisingly, considering how ubiquitous it is now, the handbag wasn't accepted with universal cries of delight. Many people complained that they looked bulky and inelegant. Others, with the casual sexism of the time, claimed that carrying something so heavy would cause injuries to women. Critics argued that they were larger than any woman needed. H.J. Cave paid no attention at first and advertised the bags until 1865, before moving their attention back to trunks. However, they still made occasional bags to special order and they were popular among the women who owned them. Slowly other manufacturers began to produce handbags too, and before long Louis decided there was a large potential market for them.

By now, Louis was firmly established at the luxury end of the market; while his luggage wasn't really any better at carrying stuff than his rivals, it had a distinctively elegant look that made it a must-have accessory for the wealthy and fashionable. Now his aim was to do the same with handbags. The first models were made from the same vivid striped canvas as his other products because he thought they would usually be bought as a matched set. However, it quickly became clear that many women who weren't looking for a set of luggage would still buy a handbag as a single item. That meant they could be made in other styles too, without worrying about matching trunks or traveling bags, and the Vuitton range quickly began to expand. In addition to canvas he began to make bags in other materials, including soft leather, and started to offer a choice of styles and sizes. Soon, fashionable women were queuing up to buy them and Louis's business received another huge boost. Not only did the introduction of handbags bring in a lot more money; it also increased his public profile. Luggage would only be used occasionally and spent most of its time in a storeroom, baggage wagon or the hold of a ship. A handbag could be used every day and taken anywhere, so it was much more visible. Even better from a business point of view, fashionable women soon decided that one bag wasn't enough. Instead they wanted a selection of them, to match different outfits, and the most fashionable of all wouldn't dream of turning up at two events with the same bag. That meant that once Louis had a customer he was almost guaranteed a steady stream of purchases.

Meanwhile Louis and Clemence-Emilie followed the trend of many wealthy people at the time and decided to send their son to school abroad. Louis had hardly any education himself but he realized the value of it. He could also recognize the importance of the increasingly wealthy USA as a market – and then there was the vast global superpower of the British Empire, which covered a quarter of the globe and had a population of close to half a billion people. If he wanted to attract more business from the English-speaking countries it seemed obvious that Georges should be educated in one of them. At the same time they didn't want him to get too far from his French heritage. In the end they found the perfect compromise - a boarding school on the island of Jersey. One of the Channel Islands, Jersey is British territory but has cultural ties to France. English and French are both official languages there, although English is the most commonly used. Its private schools attracted equal numbers of British and French students, so while Georges would get a bilingual education he wouldn't be out of his depth.

By 1875 Georges was back in Paris, living in a new house built in the grounds of the Asnières property alongside Louis's own, and Louis began teaching him how the business operated. He passed on all his own skills, but soon found that Georges was also full of ideas about how to make the Vuitton range even better. One of his innovations was to add another canvas pattern to the range. This time it was a distinctive checkered one that they named Damier, after the French word for a checkerboard. By 1888 the striped trunks were being copied by other makers, just as the Trianon gray ones had been, and Louis had decided that something needed to be done. Georges's new design was original, and hadn't been used for luggage before, so Louis was able to patent it. That gave them some extra protection against counterfeiters. Before, anyone could make a product that looked exactly like a Vuitton; now, if they did so Louis could sue them for breaching his patent. Vuitton trunks were popular enough that the sort of clients they were attracting would quickly learn what the genuine pattern looked like, so any attempt to change it just enough to get around the patent would reveal it as a copy. It was quite effective, but not completely so; counterfeits still appeared, and a few years later Georges was forced to introduce the classic LV monogram canvas with his father's initials included in the design.

By now Louis was well enough known that, when prominent people needed some special luggage, he was usually the first person they spoke to. He had an enviable reputation for producing luggage of higher quality than could be found anywhere else. After all, even before he went into business for himself his work had been good enough for the empress of France, hadn't it? Now other royalty started to buy Vuitton products. The Khedive of Egypt had been an early adopter; now King Alfonso XII of Spain was a customer.[xv] So was Alexei Nikolaevich Romanov, the heir apparent to the Russian throne (he later became Nicholas II, the last tsar of Russia). The British aristocracy, who had a simple approach to life, tended to stick with whatever (usually London-based) manufacturer their family had always used but among the fashionable Vuitton baggage was an unmistakable sign of wealth and good taste.

His products weren't just stylish, though. They were also extremely well made, and that meant that if made from the right materials they were very durable. Many of the newer items were designed for light use but even so, a combination of perfect stitching and high quality glues meant a Vuitton bag or trunk wouldn't fall apart the way a cheaper one might. That meant he attracted other types of client, too. The late 19th century was one of the great ages of exploration, and the remote corners of the world seemed to be full of wealthy European and American explorers. These scientists and adventurers often set out on expeditions that lasted years, and they needed luggage that would stand up to incredible amounts of abuse. When Louis started making canvas trunks they soon attracted attention. In addition to being lighter than leather, which was obviously a big advantage when an expedition relied on porters to carry its gear, they didn't need as much maintenance. They could survive dampness, sunlight and neglect far better than traditional luggage. It wasn't long before he started to get orders for specialized expedition gear. Medical kits, cases for scientific instruments and compact trunks began to take shape in his workshop. Some of the things explorers asked for took all his ingenuity to construct – they could be far more complex than a standard trunk or bag, but still needed to be as robust as possible. Italian explorer Pierre Savorgnan de Brazza set out to discover the source of the Congo River in 1879. He asked Louis to design and make his baggage, which included a trunk bed. These contraptions resembled a large trunk, but by pulling out a drawer and unfolding concealed panels it opened into a bed. Fitting it into the smallest possible space, and keeping it both strong enough to use and light enough to carry, was a real challenge. Earlier models made from solid timber, often covered with leather, had been immensely heavy; Louis's canvas-covered frame was much more practical and soon other expeditions were ordering them as well. He was probably the only designer whose luggage was just as much at home in the African rain forests as it was in the salons of Paris or at a party on Fifth Avenue. This reputation for practicality helped the company years later; during the First World War Georges switched production from fashionable lines to simple, robust trunks and bags that army officers could use in the trenches.

Chapter 7

Since Louis founded the company in 1857 it had been exclusively Paris-based; all his products were made there, either at Asnières or in one of the city center shops, and if you wanted to buy a Vuitton trunk or bag you had to buy it in Paris. By the 1880s, Louis had realized that needed to change. An increasing number of orders were arriving from overseas, especially from Britain, and he decided it was time to go international. It's likely that idea had been in the back of his mind for a while, and it probably influenced the decision to send Georges to school in Jersey. Louis himself sometimes found it awkward to talk to wealthy foreign customers; he struggled with English. Georges was completely different. Educated in an expensive English-speaking school, he was bilingual and completely at home in the company of the British upper class. That made the location of the first overseas Vuitton store an easy decision. In 1885 he leased a storefront at 289 Oxford Street, in London's most upmarket shopping area, and opened a branch there. Now he could compete with the top

English designers on their own turf, and now that Londoners could simply go to the store and buy Vuitton goods instead of having to write to Paris sales boomed. Georges played a major role in opening and running the London branch; he was perfectly suited to the job, and in any case, Louis was gradually handing over the day to day management of the company to him. He was now in his mid-sixties, and while he had no plans to retire he did think it was time to start thinking about the next generation of the business. Letting Georges run things in London was an ideal preparation for one day taking over completely. Meanwhile, however, there were other things that needed to be planned back in France.

The world's fair returned to Paris in 1889. The date was chosen to mark the 100th anniversary of the storming of the Bastille, the event that launched the French Revolution, and those events were chosen as the official theme. A reconstruction of the Bastille and the area around it was built, housing a ballroom where functions were held. However, another new construction dominated the exhibition, and the Paris skyline. Like the 1867 fair this one was held on the Champ de Mars, with its entrance on the bank of the Seine. Instead of a conventional gate, though, the city had commissioned a spectacular new structure. The Eiffel Tower, built for the exhibition, stood 1,063 feet above the site; it overtook the Washington Monument as the world's tallest building and could be seen from miles in every direction. Visitors going into the fair passed through the huge arch beneath its lower platform, and the energetic could walk up the steps to the third platform, 906 feet above the ground. By the time the exhibition was over nearly two million people had climbed at least part of the way up the tower.

This exhibition didn't just have a spectacular landmark to distinguish it; it was far bigger than the 1867 fair, with more than 62,000 stands, and it attracted a huge number of visitors. Between May and the end of October more than 28 million people passed under the arch of the tower to wander among the exhibits. One of those exhibits was the Vuitton stand.

Louis had expanded his range immensely since 1867. While a lot of his work was still making custom boxes for the very wealthy, he also offered an increasing number of off the shelf products. This was a great piece of forward thinking. The First World War and the social changes that followed it almost completely wiped out the custom box trade, and the manufacturers who hadn't adapted mostly went out of business. Louis was ahead of the game, though. It was still possible to arrange an appointment, have a Vuitton expert come round to measure your belongings and order custom boxes to hold them, but if you didn't want to spend quite as much you could simply walk into the shop on the Rue Scribe and take your pick from the ready-made luggage on display there.

There was plenty to choose from, too. Louis had developed a keen instinct for what people needed, and he was almost always ahead of his competitors. Long train journeys were becoming fashionable, and they were more comfortable with specialized luggage. The Orient Express was the most famous, running from Paris – later London, with the carriages loaded on a rail ferry to cross the English Channel – to Istanbul. The full journey took nearly three days so the entire train was a sleeper service, with relatively large, luxurious cabins. To make the trip as pleasant as possible Louis designed wardrobe trunks; while normal luggage was stowed in the baggage van these new trunks would be taken into the sleeper, where they opened up to act as a small but neatly laid out closet for all the clothes needed on the trip. As first class passengers would dress for dinner that was a lot more clothes than the typical modern rail passenger gets through, and Louis knew the best way to carry them. The trunks were also ideal for short sea voyages of up to a week, and by the mid-

1880s some passenger steamers were capable of crossing the Atlantic in that time.

Suitcases also experienced a rework with the Vuitton touch. Suitcases hadn't really been popular in continental Europe; they saw a lot of use among the English upper classes, but the traditional style was massively constructed and rather heavy. Most Europeans felt that if they were going to use a bulky, wood-framed piece of luggage around they'd take a trunk and hire a porter, instead of taking a suitcase and carrying it themselves. Louis has been making suitcases for years, mostly for British clients, but now he sat down and thought about it. He decided there was no reason why a suitcase *had* to be as heavy as the old-style ones. Instead of brass-bound leather over a wooden frame he started to make them from his trademark canvas, with wire stiffeners to help them stay in shape. They were an instant success. Travel was no longer just for the rich, after all; the middle class were increasingly mobile, but while they could afford rail journeys or a second-class ticket to New York they didn't have money to throw around on having trunks carried for them. A suitcase that protected their belongings but was light enough to carry comfortably was exactly what they were looking for. For anyone who hadn't seen one already, the Vuitton stand at the exhibition had plenty of them on display. It also showcased the rest of the range and some of the more ingenious items made for special orders.

Louis had done well to get a bronze medal at the 1867 exhibition but had been beaten to the top spot by older, more established manufacturers like H.L. Cave of London. This time things were different, though. He'd done more than enough to mark himself out as an unusually talented and innovative designer. His products were superbly made, extremely stylish and had more thought put into making them work, and the fair's judges took note. Louis was awarded a gold medal for the quality of his design work – especially the Damier fabric and the idea of patenting it to deter counterfeits. It was the crowning recognition of his career.

The year after the exhibition Louis introduced another refinement, a five-lever combination lock developed by Georges. Up to then most luggage had locked with simple keys; these were easily duplicated, or the lock could simply be picked. Theft was a constant problem for travelers, and the new locks did a lot to reduce it. A trunk wasn't like a modern suitcase; if a casual thief was defeated by the lock he couldn't simply slash it with a knife and get in that way. It was yet another feature that made Vuitton products more desirable than his competitors and while others quickly upgraded their own locks Louis was out in front again. In fact, the Vuittons were very creative in generating publicity about it. Georges later challenged American escape expert and illusionist Harry Houdini, who escaped from a locked trunk as part of his act, to get out of a Vuitton trunk; Houdini, he said, could be using a specially prepared box for the stunt, and getting out of a Vuitton one would be a real challenge. Houdini's reply is unknown, but as far as anyone can tell the challenge was never accepted. Of course, that doesn't mean Houdini admitted defeat – he probably wouldn't have wanted to take part in something so obviously promotional.

Louis had begun his business as a small shop servicing the needs of a small, exclusive pool of aristocratic Parisian customers. Now that he had expanded into the capital of the British Empire it had become a global company, with potential buyers right across the world. People used his luggage to travel anywhere from Australia, through India and South Africa, the West Indies and Canada as well as to French colonies in the Caribbean and North Africa; everywhere they went their stylish, practical bags and trunks were seen and admired. People wondered where they could get some too, and that represented a huge potential market. Finally, Louis decided it was time to give them a simple way to order and in 1892 the first Louis Vuitton catalogue was launched. Most luggage makers at the time didn't bother with one; as they only sold a limited range of products it wasn't worth it. For Louis it was. His range now included handbags, the full range of conventional luggage and a host of specialized items – no matter what sort of traveler you were, if you had the budget for it, there was a Louis Vuitton product that was exactly what you needed. In 35 years, the former farm boy from the Jura district had risen to the top of one of the western world's most respected professions, and established a legacy that still matters today.

Chapter 8

Louis Vuitton died at home in Asnières on February 27, 1892. What he died of isn't recorded but most likely it was simple old age. He was 70 years old and a Frenchman born in 1821 had an average life expectancy of only 55 years, so his death certainly wasn't unusually young for that time. His wife and son were with him at the end, and afterwards he was buried in the picturesque Old Cemetery at Asnières, in what's now the Vuitton family tomb.[xvi]

After Louis died the running of the company passed entirely to Georges. He continued his father's innovations, bringing in the classic monogrammed pattern in 1896 in yet another attempt to deter counterfeiters. It featured a brown background decorated with beige stars and flowers, with the entwined initials LV repeated through it as a tribute to Louis. It's been in production ever since as one of the company's signature styles.

Georges also continued the process his father had begun of turning the company into an international business. In 1893 the world's fair was held in Chicago, and there was a Louis Vuitton stand there. Three years later, to coincide with the launch of the monogram canvas, Georges toured the USA exhibiting the company's products and starting to build a network of distributors. Vuitton stores soon opened in New York and Washington, as well as other international capitals – Bombay (now Mumbai), Buenos Aires and Alexandria. The centrepiece was a huge new Paris store on the Champs-Élysées, which at the time was the largest travel goods specialist in the world. In addition to Vuitton luggage it sold clothing and accessories suitable for touring or long voyages. Other new products included the steamer bag, a small bag designed to fit inside a Vuitton trunk. Automobiles were starting to appear and, recognizing that they would revolutionize traveling, Georges designed new trunks for them. Most early automobiles didn't have dedicated load space, and luggage was usually strapped to a rack at the rear; the Vuitton trunks were built to fit in with the body shape of the most popular models, as well as giving the contents extra protection from wind, rain and road grime. The name "trunk" still survives in the USA and Jamaica for a car's load space, although it's not clear why the rest of the English-speaking world says "boot" instead. Other innovations for touring cars included compact iceboxes, picnic canteens and lightweight bags.[xvii]

The company remained as a family business after Georges died in 1936, with control passing to Louis's grandson Gaston-Louis. Shortly after that was one of the less proud periods of the firm's history. After Germany invaded France in 1940 the Vuitton family collaborated with the Germans and their Vichy puppet regime. This policy would have horrified Louis, who had suffered from German invasion himself, but his great-grandson Henry was given a medal by the pro-Nazi government for his loyalty and support to their cause. Most of the company records from 1930 to 1945 are missing, claimed to have been destroyed in a fire, but the evidence suggests that Gaston-Louis told his son to form links with the Vichy regime to help ensure the company wasn't harmed by the war.[xviii] Henry just happened to be a regular at a café where the local Gestapo had their morning coffee, so he was ideally placed to ingratiate himself with the Nazi occupiers as well as their French puppets.

It's understandable that the Vuitton family was worried about the effect of the war on the business; during the First World War they'd made folding stretchers for the French Army as well as military trunks, and they'd also been threatened with a repeat of the 1871 German occupation. In 1918 the last German offensive had gotten to less than forty miles outside Paris and the factory had been within range of the huge Paris Guns, which could fire over 80 miles. The huge shells, which reached a height of 25 miles before descending into the city – they were the first man-made objects to reach the stratosphere – killed or wounded several hundred Parisians in the summer of 1918 and the atmosphere at Asnières was tense; nobody knew when one of the massive projectiles might hit them. It also became difficult to get materials as the enemy approached. The Vuitton fortune depended on keeping the factories running so it was natural for them to avoid problems during the Second World War occupation. Most French businesses tried to work around the situation.

The Vuittons, however, crossed the line into active collaboration; they even set up a new factory to produce commemorative busts and other memorabilia of the Vichy leader, Marshal Petain. It's no surprise that after the war they tried to airbrush the whole period out of their records. They also probably knew that Louis Vuitton himself would have been ashamed of them.

With the war behind them the company continued to grow, constantly innovating with new designs and materials, until in 1987 it merged with Hennessy and Moët & Chandon, to form the luxury goods giant LVMH. Louis Vuitton products are still branded and sold separately, though, and there's now a network of more than 130 stores around the world. The latest expansion was into China; the country has a rapidly growing middle class with a huge appetite for luxury goods, and opening a store to sell genuine Vuitton products is also a tactic the company has used against counterfeiting hot spots before.

Today the main factory is still in Asnières, on a street that's now been renamed Rue Louis Vuitton. The location's the same but the factory itself has changed beyond all recognition; materials are cut by computer-controlled lasers, although most of the work is still done by hand. Trunks and suitcases are made using the same techniques that Louis himself used in the 1860s, hand-assembled by skilled craftsmen. They still aim firmly at the luxury end of the market and work hard to get celebrity endorsements for their products – stars who have appeared in LV marketing campaigns include David Bowie, Madonna and Angelina Jolie. It seems to be working, too – there are now 460 stores around the world and the company is consistently one of the world's largest designer brands.[xix]

Conclusion

There's no doubt that Louis Vuitton, the semi-literate peasant boy from Anchay, revolutionized the luggage industry and broke free of many traditional ideas that were still followed just because that's the way things had always been done. Trunks were covered in leather because… well, they just were. It took someone with vision, who wasn't afraid to take a risk and try something new, to change that. It's not as if canvas was a new product when Louis introduced his iconic slat trunk – it had been used to make tents, sails and many other items for hundreds of years. Any trunk maker could have started using it, because the advantages were obvious to anyone who looked – but none of them did. It took Louis to do that, and once he started down that road it made many other things possible. People started to get used to luggage that was available in a choice of styles, that was easier to handle and could be relied on to protect their belongings. The older manufacturers found themselves with a stark choice – follow the lead of the French upstart, or watch their customers evaporate. Most of them chose to follow, and as Louis's descendants continue to innovate and push standards ever higher, they're still following today.

In many ways, Louis invented the modern concept of a designer brand. It was his son Georges who created the famous LV monogram that makes Vuitton products so distinctive today, and that most fashion experts agree was the first actual designer label, but Louis himself had started the company down that road. Older baggage makers, like his mentor Marechal, had attracted customers through building a reputation for quality work and good service. That reputation spread through word of mouth and the patronage of influential clients. Louis changed all that; starting with the gray canvas slat trunk his products looked distinctly different and almost advertised themselves. People didn't buy Vuitton baggage because a friend had recommended it – they bought it because they'd seen it and been won over by its looks.

Louis also symbolized the changes that took place in France as it reformed itself in the wake of the Revolution. Centuries of neglect by a corrupt royal family had left the nation deeply divided on class lines, and then the bloodbath of the Revolution and the brutal rule of Napoleon Bonaparte had created a deep legacy of hatred and bitterness. With his poor background and upper class clients, Louis bridged the gap between those at the top and those at the bottom. In rising from poverty to become wealthy he showed that, if you had the talent and determination, you were no longer trapped in the class you'd been born into.

The next time you see the LV logo on a suitcase, handbag or pair of shoes it's worth remembering that those two entwined letters mean a lot more than an expensive price tag. They're a symbol of one man's struggle to escape from hardship and give people something new and exciting. Louis Vuitton defies categories; he wasn't happy to be a farm hand and was much more than simply a fashion designer. He was a shining example of what we can achieve if we really want to.

[i] GQ (July 12, 2012); *King Louis*
  http://www.gq-magazine.co.uk/style/articles/2012-07/12/louis-vuitton-history-of-luxury-label-and-outlets-shops-bags-shoes

[ii] Institut National d'études démographiques; *Life expectancy In France*
  http://www.ined.fr/en/everything_about_population/graphs-maps/interpreted-graphs/life-expectancy-france/

[iii] Vogue (June 21, 1012); *Who's Who: Louis Vuitton*
  http://www.vogue.co.uk/spy/biographies/louis-vuitton

[iv] Vogue (June 21, 1012); *Who's Who: Louis Vuitton*
  http://www.vogue.co.uk/spy/biographies/louis-vuitton

[v] Encyclopedia.com; *Louis Vuitton*
  http://www.encyclopedia.com/topic/Louis_Vuitton.aspx

[vi] GQ (July 12, 2012); *King Louis*
  http://www.gq-magazine.co.uk/style/articles/2012-07/12/louis-vuitton-history-of-luxury-label-and-outlets-shops-bags-shoes

[vii] GQ (July 12, 2012); *King Louis*
  http://www.gq-magazine.co.uk/style/articles/2012-07/12/louis-vuitton-history-of-luxury-label-and-outlets-shops-bags-shoes

[viii] Getty Images; *Georges Vuitton*
  http://www.gettyimages.com/detail/news-photo/georges-vuitton-son-of-louis-vuitton-with-his-wife-news-photo/89869248

[ix] Fashionata (Nov 8, 2011); *Louis Vuitton family home in*

Asnières
http://www.fashionata.com/fashion-my-outfit/louis-vuitton-family-home-asni%C3%A8res

[x] Biography.com; *Louis Vuitton*
http://www.biography.com/people/louis-vuitton-17112264#synopsis

[xi] The Geographical Journal, Mar 3, 1915; *Obituary – Sir George Nares*

[xii] Vogue (June 21, 1012); *Who's Who: Louis Vuitton*
http://www.vogue.co.uk/spy/biographies/louis-vuitton

[xiii] Caroline Fichiers; *1870 Menu*
http://fdlj.pagesperso-orange.fr/lettres%20de%20Caroline_fichiers/image079.jpg

[xiv] Biography.com; *Louis Vuitton*
http://www.biography.com/people/louis-vuitton-17112264#synopsis

[xv] Encyclopedia.com; *Louis Vuitton*
http://www.encyclopedia.com/topic/Louis_Vuitton.aspx

[xvi] Find A Grave; *Louis Vuitton*
http://www.findagrave.com/cgi-bin/fg.cgi?page=gr&GRid=37045393

[xvii] Encyclopedia.com; *Louis Vuitton*
http://www.encyclopedia.com/topic/Louis_Vuitton.aspx

[xviii] The Guardian (Jun 3, 2004); *Louis Vuitton's links with Vichy regime exposed*

http://www.theguardian.com/world/2004/jun/03/france.secondworldwar

[xix] Bloomberg, May 22, 1012; *Louis Vuitton Tops Hermes as World's Most Valuable Luxury Brand*
http://www.bloomberg.com/news/2012-05-21/louis-vuitton-tops-hermes-as-world-s-most-valuable-luxury-brand.html